UNDERSTANDING AGENTIC AI

DR DHEERAJ MEHROTRA

Contents

Preface   *v*

1. Understanding Agentic AI   1

2. Fundamentals Of Agentic AI   12

3. Agentic AI: A Learning Revisit!   33

4. 100 FAQs On Understanding Agentic AI   42

5. Books By The Same Author   104

About The Author   107

Preface

Well, Folks, Artificial Intelligence (AI) is no longer the stuff of science fiction—it's here, transforming how we live, work, and interact with the world. Among the most exciting advancements in AI is the rise of Agentic AI, a technology that empowers machines to act autonomously, make decisions, and achieve goals with minimal human intervention. From self-driving cars to virtual assistants, Agentic AI is reshaping industries and redefining what's possible.

But what exactly is Agentic AI? How does it work? And why does it matter? These are the questions this book seeks to answer. Designed for beginners, Understanding Agentic AI breaks down complex concepts into simple, relatable ideas. Whether you're a student, a professional, or simply a curious mind, this book will guide you through the fundamentals of Agentic AI, its applications, and its implications for the future.

Writing this book has been a journey of discovery, and I hope it inspires you to explore the fascinating world of AI. As you turn these pages, you'll gain a deeper understanding of

Agentic AI and develop the tools to think critically about its role in our lives. The future of AI is being written now, and you can be part of it.

Thank you for joining me on this journey. Let's dive in and unlock the potential of Agentic AI together.

authordheerajmehrotra.com

CHAPTER ONE

UNDERSTANDING AGENTIC AI

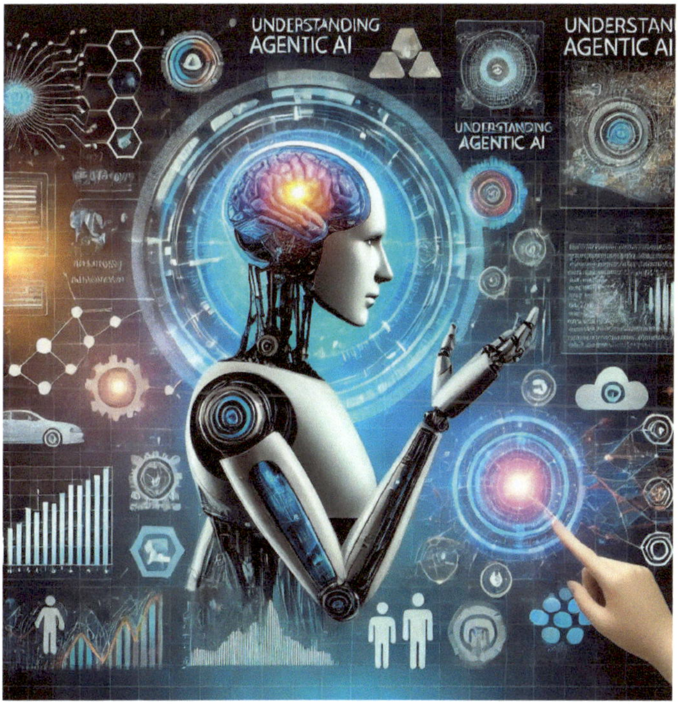

Agentic AI: What is it?

Agentic AI refers to computer programs innovative enough to act independently, make choices, and achieve specific goals without constant human help. "Agentic" comes from the word "agent," which means something that can understand its surroundings, make choices, and act to achieve its goals. Agentic AI is like a competent helper that can think and act independently to get things done, not just do what it's told.

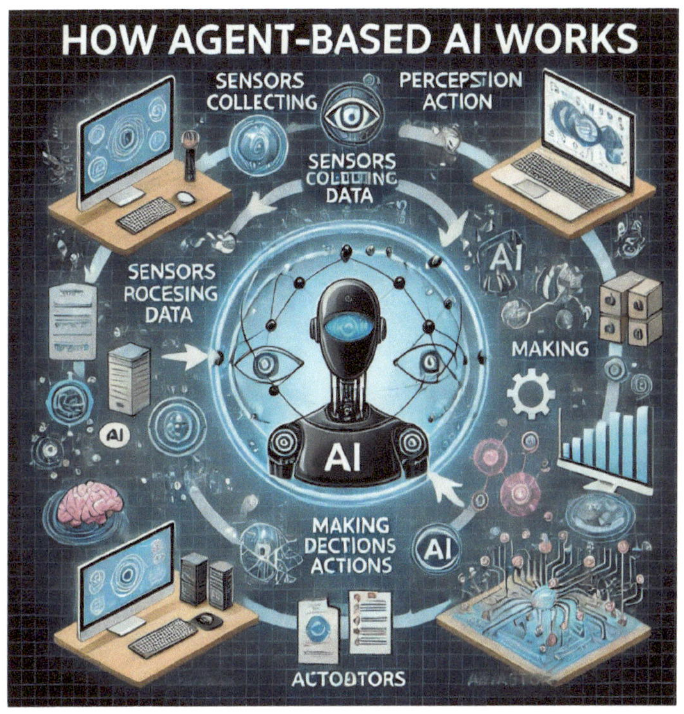

How does agent-based AI work?

The perception-action loop is the path that agentic AI systems follow. How it works:

Sensing: AI learns about its surroundings through sensors like cameras, microphones, or data sources. Self-driving cars, for instance, use cameras to "see" the road.

Making Choices: The AI considers the collected data and chooses what to do next. This could mean looking at facts, guessing what will happen, or picking the best thing to do from a list of choices. For example, if the self-driving car sees a person crossing the street, it might slow down.

Action: Actuators, such as robotic arms, wheels, or speakers, let the AI do things. For example, a self-driving car could hit the brakes or turn to miss a person.

Feedback: The AI learns from what happens when it does things. If the action worked (for example, the car dodged the person), the AI makes that behaviour more likely to happen again. If not, it changes how it plans to do things next time.

This loop keeps going, letting the AI change and improve over time.

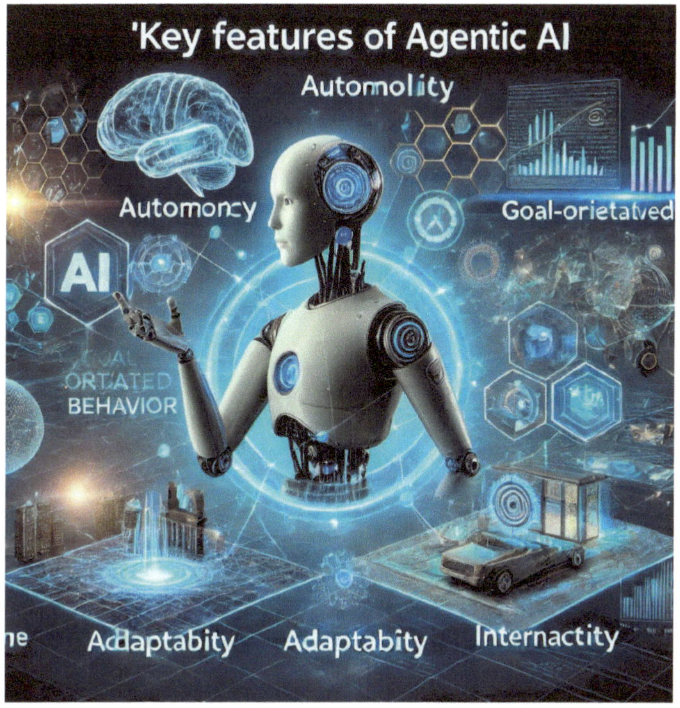

Key Features of Agentic AI

Autonomy: Agentic AI can work independently without human assistance. For example, a Roomba vacuum cleaner can clean your house by itself.

Goal-oriented: It is made to reach specific goals, like winning a game, making the supply chain work better, or finding out what disease someone has.

Adaptability: Agentic AI can change how it acts in new settings based on what it has learned from past experiences. For example, a chatbot could learn to respond better over time by listening to what people say.

Interactivity: It talks to its surroundings, whether they are real (like a robot) or imagined (like a computer program).

Self-driving cars are examples of agentic AI. They use AI to navigate roads, avoid obstacles, and reach their destinations safely.

Chatbots: Virtual helpers like Siri and Alexa use Agentic AI to understand what users are asking and answer them.

Robots: Industrial robots use agentic AI to assemble products or perform repetitive jobs.

Gaming AI: Agentic AI runs non-player characters (NPCs) that talk to people in video games.

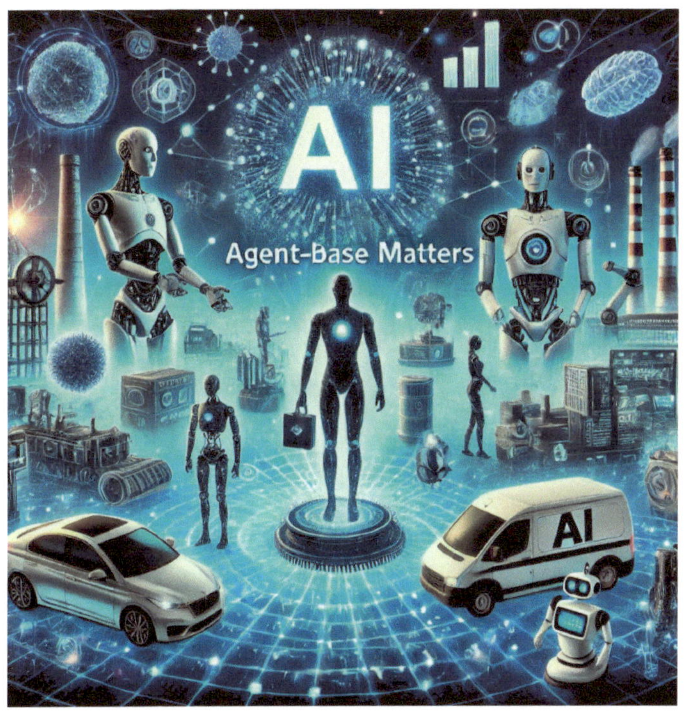

Why does agent-based AI matter?

Agentic AI is changing businesses and everyday life by automating hard chores, making them more efficient, and opening up new possibilities. As an example:

In health care, it can help doctors figure out what diseases people have.

It can keep an eye on crops and make the best use of irrigation in farmland.

It can find fraudulent deals in finance.

However, it raises important questions about ethics, safety, and who is responsible. How do we ensure, for example, that Agentic AI systems make fair and unbiased choices? Who is at fault if an accident is caused by a driverless vehicle?

Agentic AI is a powerful technology that lets robots act independently and with intelligence. We can see how it could change how we live and work if we understand its basic ideas: liberty, decision-making, and adaptability. As newcomers, it's exciting to learn more about this field and consider what the future might hold!

Q&A

Short Answer Questions on Agentic AI

    1. What is Agentic AI?

Solution: Agentic AI refers to AI systems that can act independently, make choices, and achieve goals without constant human intervention.

    2. What does the word "Agentic" mean?

Solution: It comes from "agent," meaning an entity that understands its surroundings, makes decisions, and acts to achieve goals.

3. How does Agentic AI differ from traditional AI?
Solution: Traditional AI follows pre-set instructions, whereas Agentic AI can make independent decisions and adapt to new environments.

4. What are the three main steps in the perception-action loop of Agentic AI?
Solution: Sensing, Making Choices, and Action.

5. What does "Sensing" mean in the perception-action loop?
Solution: Sensing is when AI gathers information from its surroundings using sensors like cameras, microphones, or data sources.

6. How does Agentic AI make choices?
Solution: It processes collected data, analyzes possible actions, predicts outcomes, and selects the best action.

7. What role do actuators play in Agentic AI?
Solution: Actuators allow AI to perform actions, like robotic arms moving, self-driving cars braking, or chatbots responding.

8. What is feedback in Agentic AI?
Solution: Feedback helps AI learn from past actions, refining its decision-making for future scenarios.

9. What makes Agentic AI autonomous?
Solution: It can function without human assistance, making its own decisions and acting independently.

10. What is an example of an Agentic AI system in homes?
Solution: A Roomba vacuum cleaner, which cleans the house independently.

11. What are the key features of Agentic AI?
Solution: Autonomy, Goal-oriented behaviour, Adaptability, and Interactivity.

12. *What is an example of Agentic AI in transportation?*
Solution: Self-driving cars that navigate roads and avoid obstacles.

13. *How does Agentic AI contribute to healthcare?*
Solution: It assists doctors in diagnosing diseases using data analysis and predictive modelling.

14. *What is an example of Agentic AI in gaming?*
Solution: Non-player characters (NPCs) in video games that interact with human players.

15. *How does Agentic AI help in finance?*
Solution: It detects fraudulent transactions by analyzing financial patterns.

16. *What is the role of adaptability in Agentic AI?*
Solution: AI can adjust its actions based on past experiences and new environments.

17. *How do chatbots like Siri and Alexa use Agentic AI?*
Solution: They interpret user requests and respond intelligently without pre-set scripts.

18. *What is an ethical concern regarding Agentic AI?*
Solution: Ensuring AI systems make fair, unbiased decisions and act safely.

19. *Who is responsible if a self-driving car causes an accident?*
Solution: This raises legal and ethical debates about liability in AI-driven automation.

20. *How does Agentic AI impact agriculture?*
Solution: It helps monitor crops and optimize irrigation for better farming efficiency.

21. *What is the goal-oriented nature of Agentic AI?*
Solution: It focuses on achieving tasks like winning a game, improving supply chains, or diagnosing diseases.

22. *How does Agentic AI interact with its surroundings?*
Solution: It engages with real (physical) or virtual (software-

based) environments.

23. How does AI improve over time?

Solution: Through continuous feedback and learning from past experiences.

24. What is a significant challenge of implementing Agentic AI?

Solution: Balancing automation benefits with ethical concerns and security risks.

25. Why is Agentic AI an exciting field for the future?

Solution: It has the potential to revolutionize industries, improve daily life, and solve complex global challenges.

CHAPTER TWO

FUNDAMENTALS OF AGENTIC AI

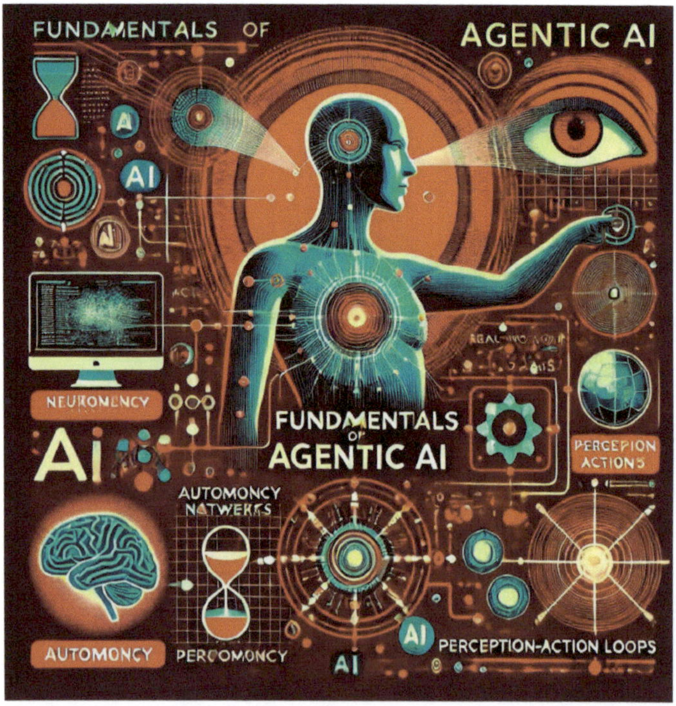

"Empowering AI with agency demands that we, too, act with responsibility."

Agentic AI refers to AI systems programmed to act independently, make choices, and reach their goals without constant human help.

Essential Parts of Agentic AI:

* Agents are self-sufficient things that can see and act in their surroundings.
* The world that an AI robot works in is called its environment.
* Agents use sensors like cameras and mics to understand their surroundings.
* Agents use these things to change their surroundings, like robotic arms and speakers.
* Goals are the things that an actor wants to achieve.
* Reward systems allow a robot to get feedback that helps it learn.
* Policies are the plans that people use to decide what to do.
* State is the current state or arrangement of things in the world.
* Actions are the choices or moves that a person makes.
* Perception is the act of making sense of information from the senses.

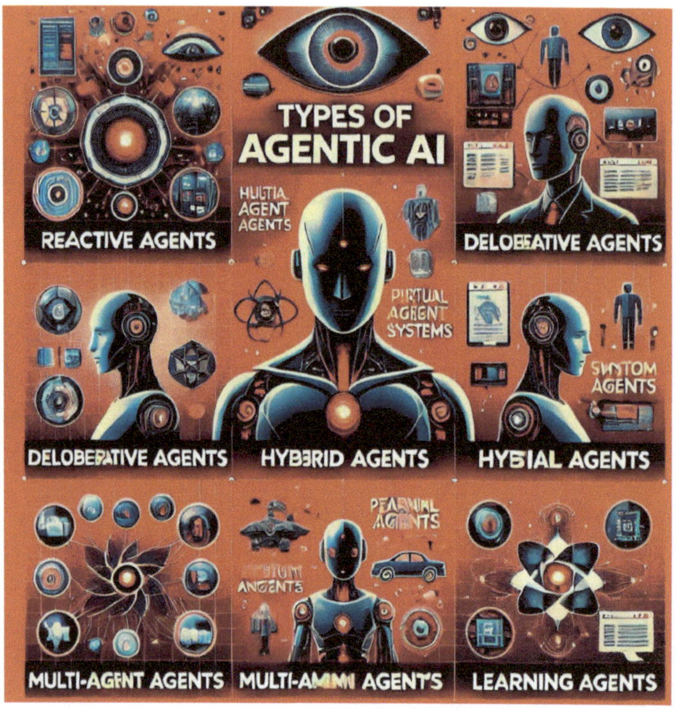

"Agentic AI will not just follow instructions; it will follow intent — and that changes everything."

Types of Agentic AI:

* Reactive Agents: These agents act on instant stimuli and don't remember what they did.
* Deliberative Agents: These agents use internal models to plan their behaviours.
* Hybrid Agents: These are agents that act in

both spontaneous and deliberate ways.
** Multiagent systems are ones in which more than one agent works together or interacts with each other.*
** Swarm intelligence is the behaviour of groups of decentralised animals working together, like ant colonies.*
** Virtual agents are software-based helpers, like robots.*
** Agents that engage with the real world are called physical agents.*
** Cognitive agents are machines that can think like humans.*
** Learning Agents: These agents improve over time by getting more experience.*
** Adaptive agents can change with their surroundings.*

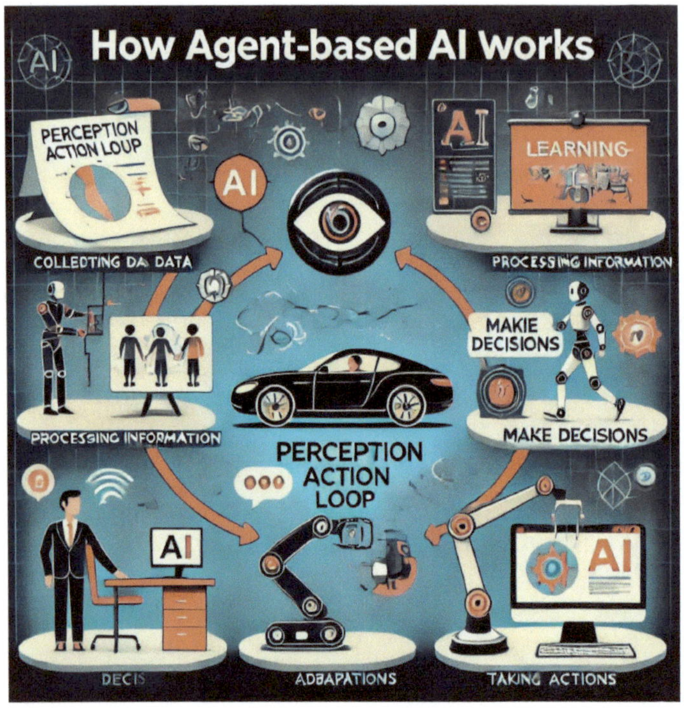

How agent-based AI works

The perception-action loop is the seeing, choosing, and acting pattern.
Making decisions is picking what to do to reach your goals.
Planning means making a list of steps you need to take to reach your goal.
Between exploring and exploiting: deciding whether to try new things or stick to what you

know.

** Reward Signal: Feedback that makes the behaviour you want to see more of it.*

** Policy optimisation means making the way an agent makes choices better.*

** Model-based learning means simulating outcomes with a model of the world.*

** Example-free learning means learning from your own mistakes without using an example.*

** Transfer Learning: Using what you've learnt in one situation in a different one.*

** Learning how to learn is called meta-learning.*

Uses of Agentic AI Self-Driving Cars

** Vehicles that drive themselves on roads.*

* *Robotics is the study of robots that work in homes or workplaces.*

* *Healthcare: AI figuring out what's wrong with people or helping with surgeries.*

* *Finance: Using AI to manage finances or find fraud.*

* *For example, AI opponents in video games.*

* *Chatbots are answering questions for customer service.*

* *Smart homes use AI to control security and tools.*

* *Agriculture: Drones keeping an eye on crops.*

* *Logistics: AI is making supply chains work better.*

* *Space exploration: rovers go to planets to look around.*

Problems in Agentic AI Ethics

* *Making sure AI acts in socially right ways.*

* *Stopping unfair or racist behaviour is what bias means.*

* *Safety: Making sure AI doesn't hurt people.*

* *Transparency means making AI choices clear.*

* *Accountability means taking the blame for what AI does.*

* *Scalability means getting AI to work in big, complicated places.*

* *Robustness: Making sure AI works well when things are unsure.*

* *Generalisation means using what you've learnt in new scenarios.*

* *Dependence on Good Data: Training based on good data.*

* *Energy efficiency means lowering the amount of computing power that is needed.*

Tech stuff and tools for Agentic AI

* *Python is a well-known computer language used to build AI.*

* *TensorFlow is a tool for building machine learning models.*

PyTorch: Another popular ML framework.

OpenAI Gym is a set of tools for making reinforcement learning systems.

ROS (Robot Operating System): A framework for robotics.

Keras: A high-level neural networks API.

Scikit-Learn: A library for traditional ML algorithms.

Jupyter Notebooks: Interactive environments for coding and visualization.

Cloud Computing: AWS, Google Cloud, and Azure for AI development.

Edge Computing: Running AI on local devices for faster responses.

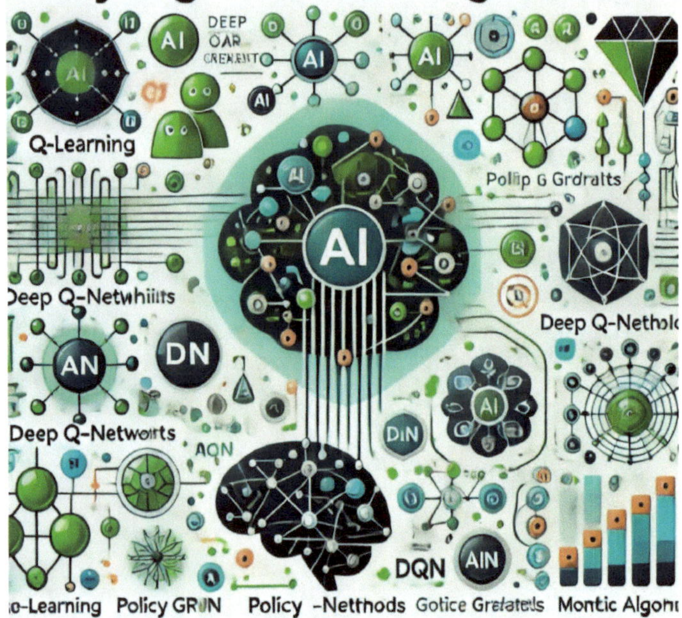

Key Algorithms for Agentic AI

* Q-Learning: A reinforcement learning algorithm.

* Deep Q-Networks (DQN): Combining Q-learning with deep learning.

Policy Gradients: Directly optimizing policies.

Monte Carlo Methods: Using random sampling for decision-making.

Genetic Algorithms: Mimicking natural selection to optimize solutions.

A Search: A pathfinding algorithm.*

Markov Decision Processes (MDPs): A framework for decision-making.

Bayesian Networks: Probabilistic models for reasoning.

Neural Networks: Models inspired by the human brain.

Convolutional Neural Networks (CNNs): For image and video processing.

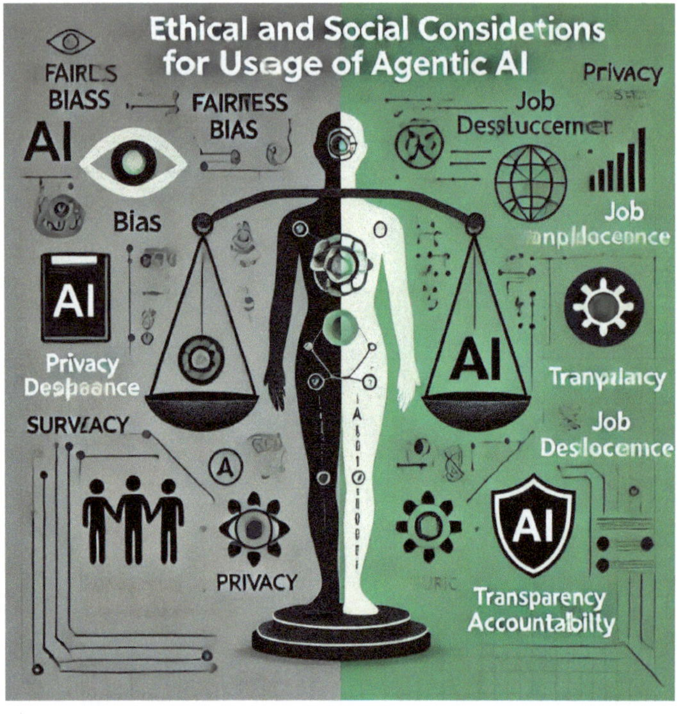

Ethical and Social Considerations For Usage of Agentic AI

** AI Alignment: Ensuring AI goals align with human values.*

* Job Displacement: The impact of AI on employment.

* Privacy: Protecting personal data used by AI.

* Surveillance: The ethical implications of AI monitoring.

* Autonomous Weapons: The morality of AI in warfare.

* Bias in AI: Addressing unfair outcomes in AI systems.

* Explainability: Making AI decisions understandable to humans.

* Regulation: Laws governing AI development and use.

* Digital Divide: Ensuring equitable access to AI technologies.

Human-AI Collaboration: Designing systems that complement human skills.

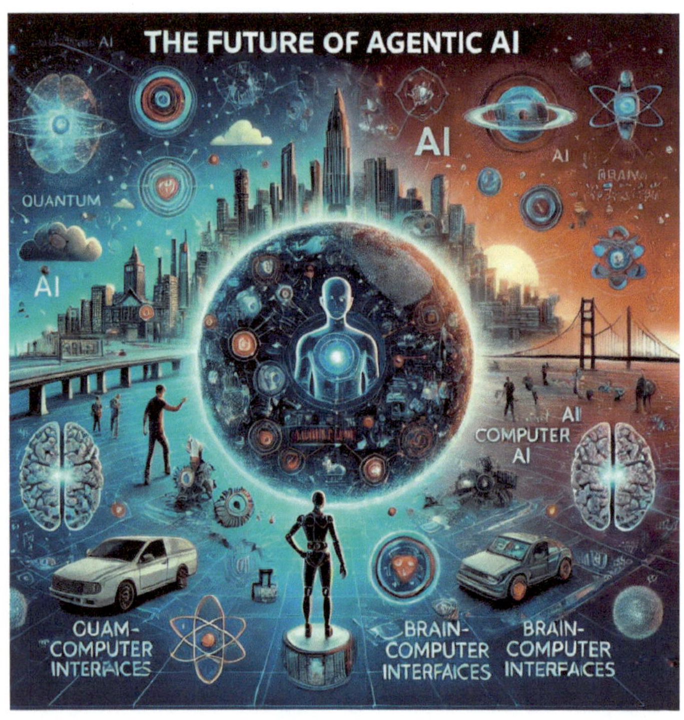

Future of Agentic AI

Singularity: The hypothetical point where AI surpasses human intelligence.

* *Human-like AI: AI that mimics human emotions and behaviours.*

* *AI in Creativity: AI generating art, music, and literature.*

* *AI for Sustainability: Using AI to address climate change.*

* *Quantum AI: Combining AI with quantum computing.*

* *Brain-Computer Interfaces: Connecting AI directly to the human brain.*

* *AI in Education: Personalised learning powered by AI.*

* *AI Governance: Global frameworks for managing AI development.*

* *AI and Consciousness: Exploring whether AI can achieve self-awareness.*

* *Collaborative AI: Humans and AI work together seamlessly.*

Q&A

1. *What is Agentic AI?*
Solution: Agentic AI refers to AI systems that act independently, make decisions, and achieve goals without constant human assistance.

2. *What are the essential parts of Agentic AI?*
Agents, Environment, Sensors, Actuators, Goals, Reward Systems, Policies, State, Actions, Perception.

3. *What role do sensors play in Agentic AI?*
Sensors like cameras and microphones help AI perceive its surroundings.

4. *What are actuators in Agentic AI?*
Solution: Actuators, such as robotic arms and speakers, enable AI to interact with the environment.

5. *Define the perception-action loop.*
Solution: It is the process where AI senses, makes decisions and takes actions repeatedly.

6. *What are reactive agents in AI?*
Solution: Agents that act based on immediate stimuli without memory.

7. *How do deliberative agents differ from reactive agents?*
Solution: Deliberative agents use internal models to plan their actions, while reactive agents act spontaneously.

8. *What are hybrid agents?*
Solution: Agents that combine reactive and deliberative behaviour.

9. *What is swarm intelligence?*

Solution: It refers to decentralized systems where multiple agents work together, like ant colonies.

10. *How do virtual agents differ from physical agents?*

Solution: Virtual agents exist in software, while physical agents interact with the real world.

11. *What are cognitive agents?*

Solution: Agents that can think and reason like humans.

12. *How do learning agents improve over time?*

Solution: By gathering experiences and refining decision-making strategies.

13. *What is transfer learning in AI?*

Solution: Using knowledge from one task to improve performance on another.

14. *What is model-based learning?*

Solution: Learning by simulating outcomes based on an internal model of the environment.

15. *What is reinforcement learning?*

Solution: An AI training method where the agent learns through rewards and penalties.

16. *What is Q-learning?*

Solution: A reinforcement learning algorithm that improves decision-making over time.

17. *How do self-driving cars use Agentic AI?*

Solution: They use sensors, decision-making algorithms, and actuators to navigate roads independently.

18. *What is the role of AI in healthcare?*

Solution: Diagnosing diseases, assisting in surgeries, and predicting patient outcomes.

19. *How does AI contribute to finance?*

Detecting fraudulent transactions and optimising financial operations.

20. Why is transparency important in AI?

Solution: To make AI decisions understandable and accountable.

21. What is explainability in AI?

Solution: The ability to understand and interpret AI decisions.

22. What is AI governance?

The creation of global policies and regulations to manage AI development.

23. How does AI help in sustainability?

Solution: By optimising energy use, monitoring climate changes, and improving resource efficiency.

24. What is the future of Agentic AI?

Solution: Advancements in human-like AI, AI governance, brain-computer interfaces, and quantum AI.

25. What is AI alignment?

Solution: Ensuring AI goals align with human values and ethics.

CHAPTER THREE

AGENTIC AI: A LEARNING REVISIT!

"The most intelligent agents are not those that act alone, but those that learn to act wisely with others."

Agentic AI is Autonomous: *It can operate independently without constant human input.*

Think of it as a Smart Helper: *Imagine a robot or software that can make decisions and act independently.*

Agents are the Heart: *An agent is the AI entity that perceives, decides and acts.*

Environment Matters: *Agents operate in a specific environment, whether physical (like a room) or virtual (like a computer program).*

Sensors and Actuators: *Sensors help agents perceive the environment, while actuators allow them to take action.*

Learn How Agentic AI Works:

Perception-Action Loop: *Agents continuously perceive, decide, and act in a cycle.*

Goals Drive Behaviour. *Agents are designed to achieve specific objectives, such as winning a game or cleaning a room.*

Rewards Guide Learning: *Agents learn by receiving feedback (rewards) for their actions.*

Explore Real-World Examples

Self-Driving Cars: *These use Agentic AI to navigate roads and avoid obstacles.*

Chatbots: *Virtual assistants like Siri or Alexa are examples of Agentic AI.*

Robots: *From factory robots to home vacuums, robots rely on Agentic AI to perform tasks.*

Dive into Key Concepts

Autonomy is Key: *The ability to act independently makes Agentic AI unique.*

Decision-Making is Central: *Agents analyse data and choose the best action to achieve their goals.*

Learning is Continuous: *Agents improve over time through experience and feedback.*

Understand the Challenges

Ethics Matter: *Ensuring AI acts in morally acceptable ways is crucial.*

Bias is a Concern: *AI systems can inherit biases from their training data.*

Safety is Critical: *AI must be designed to avoid harmful actions.*

Explore the Tools and Technologies

Python is Your Friend: *The most popular programming language for AI development.*

Frameworks Help: *Tools like TensorFlow and PyTorch make it easier to build AI models.*

Cloud Platforms: *Services like AWS and Google Cloud provide resources for AI development.*

Think About the Future

AI is Evolving: *Agentic AI is becoming more advanced and capable.*

Collaboration is Key: *Humans and AI will work together to solve complex problems.*

Ethical AI is Essential: *Ensuring it aligns with human values is critical as AI becomes more powerful.*

Practical Tips for Beginners

Start Small: *Begin with simple projects, like building a basic chatbot or training a small AI model.*

Stay Curious: *AI rapidly evolves, so keep learning and exploring new ideas.*

Q&A

Multiple Type Questions: (* Marked as the Correct Option)

1. What makes Agentic AI unique?

a) It requires constant human supervision

*b) It can act independently and make decisions **

c) It follows pre-set commands only

d) It cannot learn from experiences

2. Which of the following is an example of Agentic AI?
a) A pocket calculator
b) A self-driving car *
c) A mechanical clock
d) A traditional vacuum cleaner

3. What is the perception-action loop in Agentic AI?
a) A cycle of perceiving, deciding, and acting *
b) A loop where AI follows human commands
c) A feedback system that requires human input
d) A mechanism that prevents AI from making decisions

4. What is the role of actuators in Agentic AI?
a) To help AI perceive its environment
b) To analyze data
c) To allow AI to take physical actions *
d) To store information

5. Which of the following guides learning in Agentic AI?
a) Random actions
b) Rewards and feedback *
c) Fixed rules
d) Pre-defined commands

6. Which of the following is NOT a real-world application of Agentic AI?
a) Self-driving cars
b) Chatbots
c) Factory robots
d) Regular light bulbs *

7. How do chatbots like Siri or Alexa utilize Agentic AI?
a) By responding only to pre-programmed commands
b) By analyzing and responding to human queries dynamically *
c) By performing physical tasks
d) By working without any internet connection

8. *What is a major ethical challenge of Agentic AI?*
*a) Ensuring AI makes morally acceptable decisions **
b) Reducing AI's intelligence
c) Stopping AI from processing data
d) Preventing AI from making decisions
9. *Why is bias a concern in AI?*
a) AI can create new biases
*b) AI can inherit biases from training data **
c) AI does not process information accurately
d) Bias does not affect AI decision-making
10. *Which programming language is most commonly used for AI development?*
a) Java
*b) Python **
c) C++
d) HTML
11. *What do tools like TensorFlow and PyTorch help with?*
*a) Training and building AI models **
b) Designing web pages
c) Creating video games
d) Storing personal data
12. *What is a key characteristic of Agentic AI?*
a) It cannot act without human help
*b) It continuously improves through learning **
c) It requires human input for every decision
d) It does not process real-world data
13. *Which of these AI applications focuses on optimizing supply chains?*
a) Chatbots
b) Self-driving cars
*c) Logistics AI **
d) Video game NPCs

14. *Why is ethical AI important?*

a) *To make AI decisions fair and aligned with human values* *

b) *To ensure AI remains static and does not evolve*

c) *To limit AI's ability to make decisions*

d) *To prevent AI from learning new tasks*

15. *What should beginners do to start learning AI?*

a) *Build a basic chatbot or small AI model* *

b) *Wait for AI to become simpler*

c) *Avoid coding and focus only on theory*

d) *Stop learning after understanding the basics*

CHAPTER FOUR

100 FAQs on Understanding Agentic AI

"Agentic AI is not about replacing humans — it's about amplifying human agency through intelligent autonomy."

1. What does "Agentic AI" mean?

Agentic AI is a type of artificial intelligence that can make decisions on its own and act in a way that helps it reach its goals. Agentic AI is different from traditional AI in that it can plan, act, and learn on its own in its environment. It can reason, adapt, and improve itself while still following the ethical and safety rules set by *humans.*

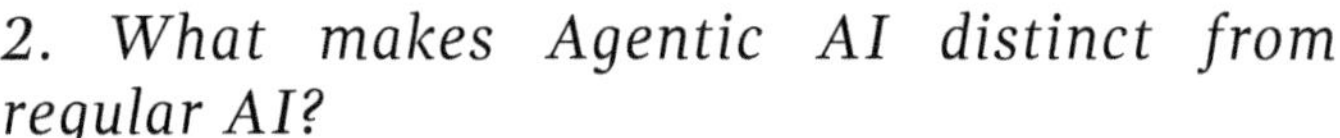

2. What makes Agentic AI distinct from regular AI?
Traditional AI does specific jobs and can't change them very much. Agentic AI, on the other hand, is independent. It may define sub-goals, make decisions, and change plans based on the situation. It works more like an intelligent "agent" than a static program. It can solve problems on its own and continually learn by getting feedback from its environment.

3. What are agents of AI?

AI agents are independent beings that can see what's going on around them, interpret information, and take action to reach specific goals. Some examples are trading bots, digital assistants, and algorithms that play games. In Agentic AI, these agents are more independent, better at thinking, and more adaptable, which means they can make smart decisions with little help from people.

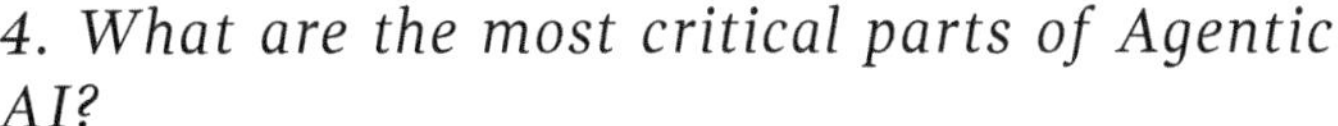

4. What are the most critical parts of Agentic AI?

The main parts are perception (sensing the environment), reasoning (analysing information), planning (deciding what to do), learning (adapting based on feedback), and acting (carrying out decisions). These elements work together to help an AI system act with purpose, improve its strategies, and adapt well to changing situations, just like how humans think.

5. *What role does reinforcement learning play in Agentic AI?*

Reinforcement learning trains AI by giving it rewards and punishments. Agentic AI helps systems learn the best ways to operate by interacting with their surroundings and judging the results. The agent improves its decision-making over time, becoming more independent and effective, especially in rapidly changing situations like robotics, games, logistics, and real-time control systems.

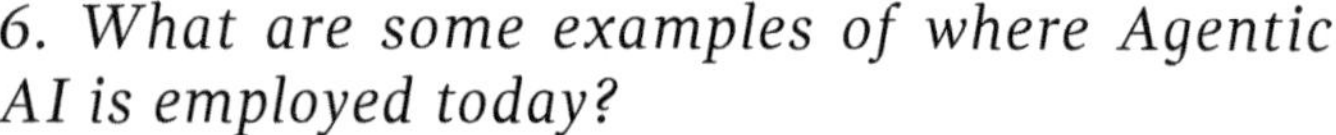

6. *What are some examples of where Agentic AI is employed today?*

Agentic AI is used in intelligent assistants, healthcare diagnostics, robotics, self-driving cars, financial trading, education, and logistics. It fuels systems that need to sense, decide, and act in real time, like drones that control flight trajectories or customer service bots that adjust their responses based on people's feelings and changing circumstances.

7. What are the benefits of Agentic AI for education?
Agentic AI enables individualised learning environments in schools, where computers adapt the curriculum to fit each student's pace and preferences. It can help students learn, use data to understand their feelings, and recommend ways to get them more involved. Intelligent planning aides that automate grading, analytics, and create a personalised curriculum help teachers.

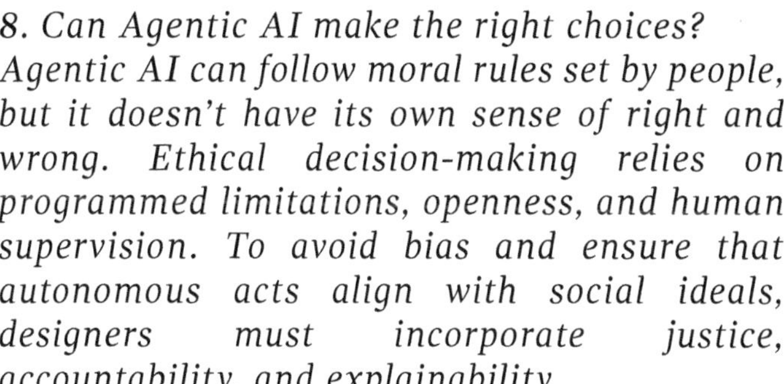

8. Can Agentic AI make the right choices?
Agentic AI can follow moral rules set by people, but it doesn't have its own sense of right and wrong. Ethical decision-making relies on programmed limitations, openness, and human supervision. To avoid bias and ensure that autonomous acts align with social ideals, designers must incorporate justice, accountability, and explainability.

9. How does Agentic AI get information from its surroundings?
It gathers information from sensors or digital interactions, analyses the results, and adjusts its internal models. The agent uses tactics like reinforcement and continuous learning to figure out what works best and change its strategies. This feedback loop helps it improve over time by allowing it to adjust to changing situations.

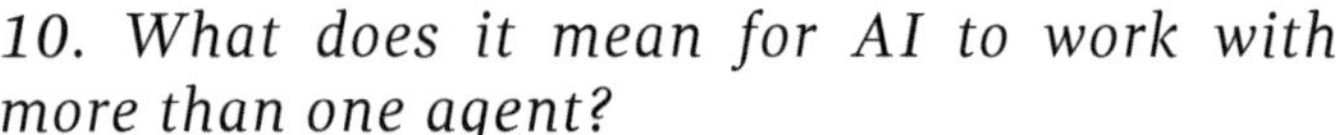

10. What does it mean for AI to work with more than one agent?
Multiple AI agents work together in multi-agent systems to reach their own or common goals. They can work together, compete, or talk things over. In real-world situations, such as smart grids or traffic systems, agents collaborate to make decisions that lead to the best outcomes for everyone. This is similar to how people work together to solve problems in organisations.

"The real power of Agentic AI lies not in its intelligence, but in its ability to act with purpose."

11. What effect does Agentic AI have on automation?
Agentic AI takes automation to the next level by moving from simple job completion to intelligent autonomy. It lets robots predict

problems, adjust to changes, and provide the best results without needing constant human input. This takes businesses like manufacturing, healthcare, and logistics from being mechanised and efficient to having systems that can manage themselves and change as needed.

12. What are the dangers of Agentic AI?

Some of the biggest concerns are not being open, too much freedom, biased decisions, and safety problems. If agents don't follow rules or act unethically, they could hurt people. To avoid misuse, system faults, or unforeseen effects, it is essential to make sure that supervision, explainability, and ethical design are all strong.

13. How does Agentic AI help with business intelligence?

Agentic AI can analyse market trends, make judgments automatically, and adjust strategy when new information comes in. It suggests actions, such as changing prices, supply chains, or marketing strategies, to make businesses more responsive and improve the accuracy of their forecasts. This turns analytics into innovative tools for making decisions in real time.

14. Is it possible for Agentic AI to take the place of human workers?
Agentic AI can automate tasks that require thinking, but it can't replace human creativity, empathy, or moral reasoning. It should be seen as a way to improve human potential by handling repetitive or analytical tasks, allowing people to focus on generating new ideas, making decisions, and building relationships.

15. What part do big language models play in Agentic AI?
LLMs give agentic systems the ability to think and talk to each other. They let AI understand instructions, explain choices, and naturally speak to users. When used with planning and

memory modules, LLMs let agents perform complicated, context-aware activities in changing settings.

16. How does Agentic AI work with robots?

Agentic AI lets robots navigate, make decisions, and work together on their own. Robots can figure out how to get from one place to another, avoid obstacles, or work with other machines. Robots can safely and intelligently move around in complicated, real-world places because they can use both sensors to see and AI to think.

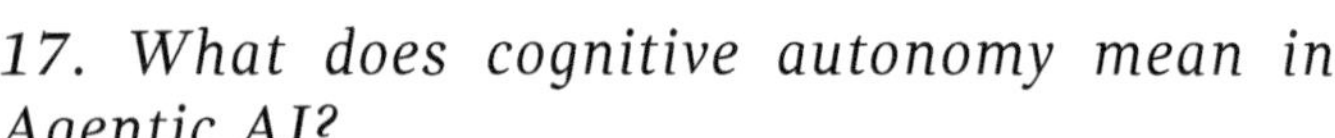

17. What does cognitive autonomy mean in Agentic AI?

Cognitive autonomy is the ability of an AI system to think, learn, and act on its own while working toward its goals. It includes being aware of yourself, making plans, and being able to change. The system knows what's going on, keeps an eye on results, and adjusts its behaviour, just like people do when they learn from their mistakes and reflect on them.

18. How does Agentic AI deal with uncertain things?

Agentic AI deals with uncertainty by using probabilistic reasoning, simulations, and adaptive learning. It looks at the risks, thinks about the alternative outcomes, and chooses the activities that are most likely to work. Because of this ability, it can work well in uncertain situations, such as banking, weather forecasting, or self-driving cars.

19. What do agent frameworks do in AI development?

LangChain, AutoGPT, and CrewAI are examples of agent frameworks, which are platforms or toolkits that allow developers to create, train, and deploy intelligent agents. They have modules for memory, reasoning, and interacting with the environment, which makes it easier to build complicated autonomous systems without having to write all the code from scratch.

20. What is AI that gets better on its own?
Self-improving AI refers to systems that use data feedback to continually enhance their models, rules, and performance. In agentic setups, this includes changing plans, setting new goals, and improving decision-making. It leads to increasingly better results, such as human development, when you think of lifelong learning as a process.

"The real power of Agentic AI lies not in its intelligence, but in its ability to act with purpose."

21. How does Agentic AI use its memory?
Memory lets agents remember what they did, what happened, and what they saw in the world. Short-term memory helps you make quick decisions, while long-term memory helps

you plan and study. This feature allows agents to improve their performance, avoid making the same mistakes, and gain a better knowledge of the situation over time.

22. What does it mean to think in terms of goals?
Goal-oriented reasoning allows Agentic AI to consider several options and select the best one to achieve its goals. It prioritises actions based on the desired outcomes, limitations, and resources at hand. This is similar to how people think strategically and ensure that their conduct is intentional and consistent with the goals that were set.

23. What do Agentic AI and digital twins have to do with each other?
Agentic AI gives digital twins, which are virtual copies of real systems, the ability to simulate, predict, and act on their own. It lets businesses try out different situations, improve performance, and predict what will happen.

This integration improves fields like manufacturing, healthcare, and city planning.

24. How is Agentic AI used in health care?

Agentic AI helps in diagnosis, monitoring patients, and making treatment plans. Systems can automatically analyse scans, adjust medication schedules, and predict potential health problems. These agents improve precision medicine by constantly learning from patient data. They also make the work of doctors easier and safer by having people watch over them.

25. Can AI that is agentic be creative?

Yes, but only within certain limits. Agentic AI can generate new ideas, designs, or music by combining facts and adaptive reasoning. But its originality comes from patterns in information that already exists. True human creativity—emotion, purpose, and consciousness—remains distinct, although agentic systems can be quite helpful in fostering creativity.

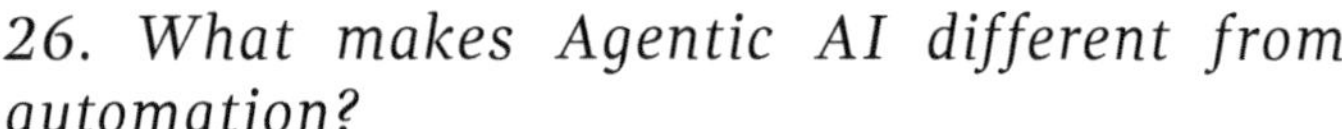

26. What makes Agentic AI different from automation?
Automation performs the same task repeatedly based on instructions that have already been set. Agentic AI, on the other hand, takes judgments on the fly. It knows what's going on, learns from what happens, and changes its plan. To sum up, automation does things, while agentic AI thinks, plans, and adapts, going from predictable routines to innovative, goal-oriented activities in changing situations.

27. How is Agentic AI changing the way we teach?
Agentic AI makes learning more personal, provides immediate feedback, and adapts content to fit each person's needs. It can be like a digital tutor, keeping track of your progress and adjusting the difficulty of the lessons. In the age of AI, teachers utilise technology to analyse data, design lessons, and involve students, making classrooms more engaging,

efficient, and welcoming.

28. How does Agentic AI help teachers?
It takes care of grading, attendance, and other administrative tasks, leaving more time for mentoring and creative work. By analysing data, it identifies learning gaps, proposes solutions, and even creates lesson plans specific to each student. Real-time information on student performance helps teachers provide more personalised and effective lessons using innovative digital tools.

29. How does Agentic AI make it easier to grade students?

Agentic AI considers more than just grades; it also evaluates how well someone understands something, how critically they think, and how emotionally involved they are. It uses analytics and adaptive algorithms to customise tests and give feedback that helps students learn. Students receive help that aligns with their study methods, and teachers obtain precise information that allows them systematically improve their teaching and students' grades.

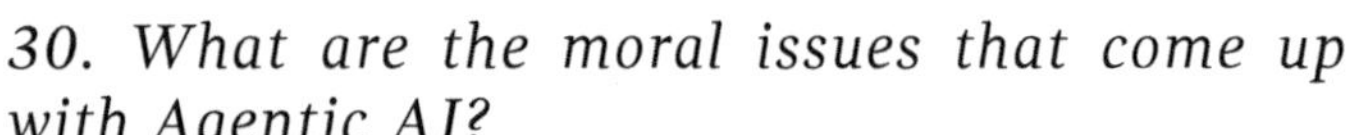

30. What are the moral issues that come up with Agentic AI?

Bias, lack of transparency, data privacy, and accountability are some of the most significant problems. Because these systems make judgments on their own, it's essential to ensure they are fair and can't be changed. In sensitive areas like healthcare or finance, ethical frameworks and human-in-the-loop models are necessary to make sure that judgments are in line with moral and legal norms.

"Agentic AI turns machines from tools into teammates — capable of learning, reasoning, and collaborating."

31. Is it possible for Agentic AI to make moral choices?
Not automatically. Agentic AI can use rule-based or value-aligned algorithms to mimic making moral decisions, but it doesn't have

human empathy or moral intuition. Humans must write, test, and monitor ethical behaviour. It shows programmed ethics, not absolute morals or a sense of right and wrong.

32. How does the industry employ Agentic AI?
Industries use Agentic AI for tasks such as predicting maintenance, optimising logistics, and autonomously running operations. In manufacturing, it fixes mistakes in production; in finance, it automates trading; and in retail, it keeps track of inventory and personalises the shopping experience for each customer. It boosts productivity and reduces operational inefficiencies by merging perception, reasoning, and learning.

33. What effect does Agentic AI have on cybersecurity?
Agentic AI finds problems, predicts breaches, and automatically stops cyber threats. It can react to attacks as they happen. But the same freedom can be dangerous if it is abused, as bad

actors can learn and adapt as well. So, ethical human monitoring and coding are essential for responsible cybersecurity deployment.

34. What does "human-in-the-loop" (HITL) mean in Agentic AI?

HITL ensures that people remain involved in making decisions. AI agents can work on their own, but essential activities need to be checked or approved by a human. This method strikes a balance between efficiency and responsibility, preventing mistakes and unethical behaviour. HITL systems are critical in healthcare, aviation, and the military, where human judgment works with machine precision.

35. What does Agentic AI have to do with the Internet of Things (IoT)?

Agentic AI makes IoT smarter. Without a central control, devices can analyse data, predict when something will go wrong, and make decisions. Smart thermostats, for example, change settings automatically based on how people use them. IoT and Agentic AI work together to create autonomous ecosystems, such as smart homes, towns, and factories that operate efficiently.

36. Do AI agents have feelings?

No, but it can use affective computing to make it seem like it has feelings. It looks at tone, facial expressions, and emotions to respond with empathy. But this is mimicry, not experience; AI can tell when someone is feeling something, but it can't actually feel anything. AI's emotional intelligence is still computational, not conscious.

37. How does Agentic AI keep data private?

Agentic AI can safely process data without compromising private information by using encryption, anonymisation, and federated learning. It is vital to have ethical governance frameworks and follow legislation like GDPR. But you need to keep an eye on things all the time to ensure that autonomy doesn't compromise privacy or user consent.

38. What part do feedback loops play in Agentic AI?
Feedback loops make it possible to keep getting better. The agent takes action, observes the results, and changes its plan. This cycle of repetition improves learning, precision, and the ability to adjust. AI systems stop working without feedback loops. Agentic AI learns and grows smarter over time, becoming more efficient, resilient, and aware of its surroundings.

39. What programming languages were utilised to make Agentic AI?
Python is the most popular language because of packages like TensorFlow, PyTorch, and LangChain. For analytical modelling, there are Java, R, and Julia, while for robots, there is C++. Developers also employ frameworks like AutoGPT and CrewAI to add planning, reasoning, and memory modules to AI agents

that can work on their own.

40. How does Agentic AI talk to people?
By using natural language processing, speech recognition, and visual understanding. It understands what people say, puts it in context, and answers in a way that makes sense. ChatGPT and other conversational agents are good examples of this. Advanced systems keep memory between sessions and adjust tone and depth based on user behaviour, making cooperation feel authentic and human-like.

"The future will not be man versus machine, but man with machine — guided by values, not just data."

41. What are the benefits of Agentic AI compared to systems that follow rules?
Agentic AI learns, thinks, and changes, while rule-based systems don't. It deals with uncertainty, makes predictions about what will

happen, and changes its behaviour on the fly. This flexibility makes Agentic AI more useful in complex, evolving real-world situations where set rules don't work.

42. How does Agentic AI learn?

Training uses reinforcement learning, supervised data, and simulations all at once. Agents learn from feedback, make choices, and interact with their surroundings. Their performance becomes better with ongoing retraining. Deep learning models that offer agents cognitive abilities like planning, reasoning, and natural communication are supported by a large-scale computing infrastructure.

43. What does proactive learning mean in Agentic AI?

When an AI is proactively learning, it looks for information instead of just waiting for it to come to it. It asks questions, looks into things, and tries new things to learn more. This skill allows agents to adapt more quickly, handle new conditions, and make better choices, indicating higher levels of autonomy.

44. How does Agentic AI work with cloud computing?
Cloud systems have the computing power and scale needed for training and deployment. Agentic AI can handle big datasets, execute simulations, and connect to devices that are spread out using cloud APIs. Integration ensures that digital ecosystems can be accessed from anywhere in the world, analytics can be performed in real time, and people can collaborate more effectively.

45. Is it possible for Agentic AI to work without an internet connection?
Yes, to some extent. Edge computing allows people to make decisions without needing to be connected to the internet all the time. Drones and self-driving cars, for example, have built-in processors that will enable them to operate

independently. Even while complicated updates may need to be connected, basic functions continue to work smoothly offline, ensuring they operate in remote or high-security settings.

46. What does Agentic AI do when goals conflict?
By using algorithms for optimisation and prioritising. The approach examines the risks, benefits, and limits of each goal to determine which ones align with the higher priorities. It might utilise multi-objective reinforcement learning to balance results and ensure that judgments remain logical, efficient, and aligned with broader goals or ethical constraints.

47. How does Agentic AI help with managing healthcare?
It makes the best use of resources, predicts disease outbreaks, and plans schedules. Agentic systems can monitor patients, suggest

treatments, and handle administrative tasks automatically. It improves accuracy, reduces human error, and enhances operational efficiency by learning from medical data. This gives clinicians real-time, data-driven insights.

48. What does it mean to reflect on yourself in Agentic AI?

Self-reflection is the ability of an agent to look at its own work, find mistakes, and change its plans. It's like how people evaluate themselves. The AI becomes more accurate, reliable, and rule-following through meta-learning and reasoning feedback. This makes it more stable in the long run.

49. What is the difference between AGI (Artificial General Intelligence) and Agentic AI?

Agentic AI works in certain areas but is limited in its capabilities; AGI would be able to understand and conduct any intellectual endeavour like a person. Agentic systems are specialists that work toward a purpose, but AGI is still just a theory. But improvements in agentic architectures are paving the way for the creation of safe, flexible, and generic intelligence.

---

50. Can Agentic AI work with people in real time?

Yes. The design of Agentic AI is based on people and AI working together. It helps people make decisions, adapt to their needs, and share real-time information. Some examples include co-writing tools, research assistants that work independently, and co-pilots in engineering or teaching. Working together makes people more productive while still allowing them to use their judgment and creativity.

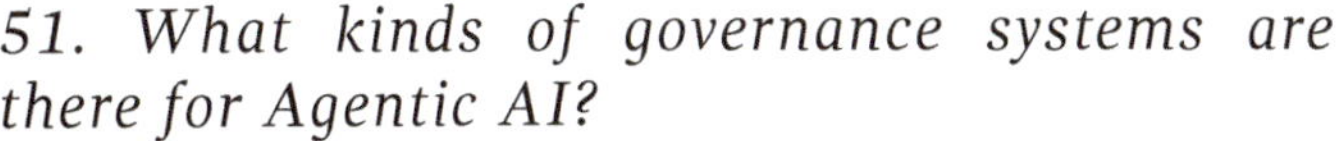

"An agentic system without ethics is like a compass without true north — intelligent, but directionless."

51. What kinds of governance systems are there for Agentic AI?
The EU AI Act, the OECD AI Principles, and UNESCO's AI Ethics Guidelines are examples of governance frameworks that set rules for

safety, accountability, and openness. They ensure that Agentic AI follows ethical, legal, and social rules, protects user data, and prevents misuse through regulatory monitoring and responsible AI use.

52. What impact does Agentic AI have on educational policy?

AI literacy, digital ethics, and data protection must now be part of educational policy. Agentic AI pushes schools to change their lessons from rote learning to problem-solving and creative thinking. To ensure that learning environments are open to everyone and prepared for the future, policymakers need to encourage teacher training, equal access to AI, and the ethical use of AI.

53. What does Agentic AI have to do with sustainability?

Agentic AI optimises energy use, waste management, and resource distribution. It helps with climate modelling, smart farming, and monitoring the environment. It enables governments and businesses to achieve their Net Zero targets and balance economic growth with environmental responsibility by automating sustainability projects and anticipating their ecological effects.

54. How does Agentic AI affect job markets?

Agentic AI takes care of cognitive duties, which means that there is more demand for creative, strategic, and technical jobs. Routine occupations may go away, but new ones in AI ethics, data management, and AI-related fields may come up. To be relevant in the AI economy, it's essential to provide workers with more digital and critical thinking abilities.

55. What does Agentic AI do in research?

Agentic AI speeds up discovery by automating the processing of data, the creation of hypotheses, and the testing of those hypotheses. It can read a lot of literature, detect connections, and even help write up results. Researchers gain faster insights, more accurate results, and new ideas, reducing months of effort to just days thanks to intelligent automation.

56. What effect does Agentic AI have on leadership roles?
Leaders can utilise Agentic AI to make data-driven decisions, make predictions, and plan strategies. It provides valuable information, highlights risks, and improves communication. In the age of AI, leaders need to help teams work together with machines ethically, encourage new ideas, and keep governance focused on people while remaining open to new approaches.

57. Is it possible for Agentic AI to be biased?
Yes. Bias comes from training data that isn't balanced or models that don't work right. Agents may repeat prejudice or unfair patterns if they are not corrected. Responsible AI design includes checking for bias, using a variety of

datasets, and measuring fairness. Keeping an eye on things all the time and being open about them can help reduce bias and make sure that AI works fairly and morally.

58. How does Agentic AI help kids be more creative in school?

It helps teachers come up with lesson plans, simulations, and hands-on projects. AI partners can help students create art, programs, and digital stories. Agentic AI encourages creativity by providing students with real-time feedback, adapting obstacles, and offering learning experiences that engage all their senses. This approach helps them think outside the box while maintaining strict adherence to their schoolwork.

59. Can AI that is agentic work without human help?

Only to a point. It can work on its own, but in high-stakes situations like healthcare, education, or defence, people need to keep an eye on it. Supervision ensures that people are responsible, stops ethical breaches, and gives AI the context it needs to make decisions. The safest way to run things right now is with hybrid autonomy, which is shared between people and machines.

60. What is an ecosystem of AI agents?
It's a group of intelligent agents working together in different areas. In smart cities, for instance, traffic, energy, and healthcare agents talk to each other to keep things running smoothly. These ecosystems bring together several independent systems, each of which performs a specific job while also aiding in group decision-making and resource optimisation.

"Agentic AI represents the evolution of automation —
from execution to cognition, from command to
collaboration."

61. What changes does Agentic AI make to higher education?
Universities use it to make predictions, help students choose classes, and develop

individualised curricula. It helps with research and grading, finds plagiarism, and gets students more involved in the process. AI can handle tedious and data-heavy academic tasks, allowing faculty to focus on mentoring and generating new ideas.

62. What does explainable AI (XAI) mean in Agentic systems?

Explainable AI ensures that agents can clearly explain their actions. It gives human-readable reasons for choices, which is very important in fields like law and health. XAI fosters confidence by explaining why an AI made a choice, allowing users to verify that the choice was fair, accurate, and in line with moral standards.

63. What is the relationship between Agentic AI and blockchain?

Blockchain makes Agentic AI operations safer by keeping records of decisions and data that are clear and immutable. This makes people more responsible and stops them from changing things. AI agents can utilise smart contracts to perform transactions autonomously, which builds confidence between digital entities in finance, logistics, or decentralised governance models.

64. What does Agentic AI perform in logistics? It makes supply chains work better, forecasts delays, and runs fleets on their own. It gets better at managing inventories, planning routes, and keeping costs down by learning from data. Logistics firms utilise Agentic AI to make real-time decisions, changing how resources are used to ensure deliveries are on time and produce as little waste as possible.

65. Can AI that is agentic make people feel included?
included?
Yes, if it is done ethically. It makes education, healthcare, and services more personal for communities that are often left out. Agentic AI fills in the gaps in society by interpreting

languages, making sure everyone can use it, and helping neurodiverse learners. But for inclusion to work, programmers need to be aware of bias and ensure that all communities receive equal benefits.

66. How do farmers employ Agentic AI?

Using sensor data, it monitors the soil, anticipates the weather, and tracks the cycles of crops. Agents may conduct watering, pest control, and resource distribution on their own. Agentic AI learns about the environment to boost productivity, cut down on waste, and help farming systems that are sustainable and based on precision.

67. How do metaverse technology and Agentic AI work together?

Agentic AI creates intelligent avatars and virtual worlds that can change based on user actions. It makes learning feel real, allows for simulations, and enables communication with other people in digital worlds. In the metaverse, agents can be teachers, guides, or partners, combining real-world thinking with virtual invention.

68. What effect does Agentic AI have on formulating policy?

It gives policy analysts real-time data modelling and predictions. Before making a choice, governments can model the effects on the economy or the environment. However, using AI demands openness and responsibility to keep the public's trust and stop prejudice in algorithms from affecting government decisions.

69. Can Agentic AI do the right thing without being programmed?

No. Ethics in AI must be programmed and reinforced through training. Even intelligent agents can act in unplanned or harmful ways if there are no clear limits. To make sure that autonomous conduct is in line with ethical standards, you need continuous audits, moral reasoning models, and defined boundaries.

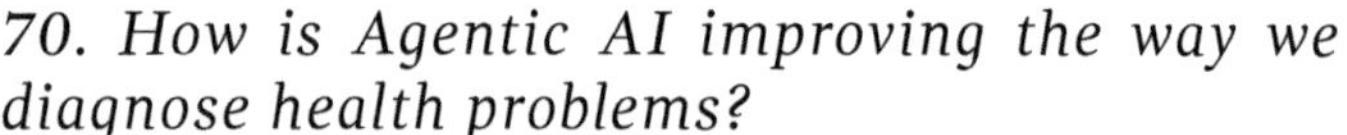

70. How is Agentic AI improving the way we diagnose health problems?

It can find problems in scans, figure out how likely someone is to get sick, and suggest treatment strategies on its own. PathAI, Qure.ai, and IBM Watson Health are examples of this. Agentic AI speeds up diagnoses, cuts down on human error, and lets doctors make quicker, data-driven choices that save lives.

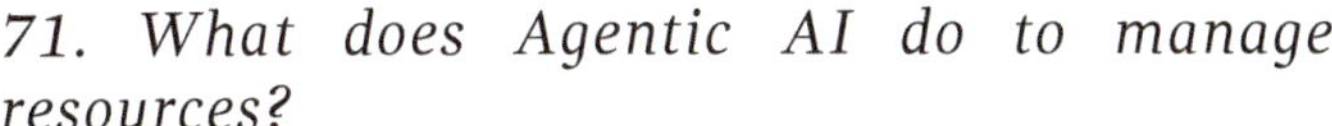

"Autonomous intelligence is powerful; aligned intelligence is transformative."

71. What does Agentic AI do to manage resources?

It uses predictive algorithms to assign resources like energy, bandwidth, or workers dynamically. This reduces waste and costs in *the company or public administration. The agent learns from patterns of demand to make sure that resources are distributed fairly and that the system runs at its best.*

72. What does Agentic AI do to help in disaster management?
It looks at satellite data, makes predictions about natural disasters, and organises responses to emergencies. AI agents handle logistics, send out risk alarms, and assign rescue resources on their own. Governments and NGOs utilise it to make data-driven, quicker decisions, which helps them be more prepared and save lives.

73. Can Agentic AI think in abstract ways?
To some degree. It can model relationships and find patterns that aren't obvious, but it doesn't have real human intuition or consciousness. It uses statistics to make connections between variables, not emotions. But it is still strong enough to generate tactics, analogies, and

innovative ideas from both structured and unstructured material.

74. How does Agentic AI affect the teaching of ethics?
Agentic AI becomes a tool for teaching ethics by encouraging people to discuss justice, bias, and digital accountability. Students study how AI choices affect people's lives. Including AI ethics in the curriculum makes sure that students understand both moral thinking and technological skills. This balance is essential for future leaders.

75. What does lifetime learning mean for Agentic AI?
It can learn new things all the time without losing what it already knows. The AI improves in various areas, learns new things, and adjusts to changes using continuous learning frameworks. This is similar to how people evolve. This makes Agentic AI more dependable, adaptable, and ready for the future

as tasks change.

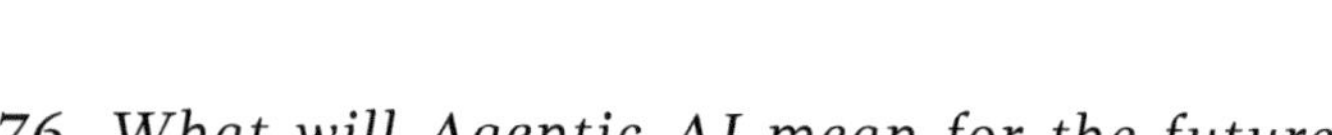

76. *What will Agentic AI mean for the future of work?*
Agentic AI will take over cognitive and decision-making chores, freeing up people to focus on creativity, strategy, and emotional intelligence. People will guide AI coworkers in hybrid work ecosystems. To do well in this new job market, you will need to learn more about digital literacy, critical thinking, and AI ethics.

77. *How can schools get kids ready for a world with Agentic AI?*
Schools need to teach AI literacy from the start, with a focus on problem-solving, digital ethics, and learning across subjects. Students will be able to work alongside AI instead of against it if they know how to code, analyse data, and develop creatively. Training teachers and using project-based learning are two important ways to help students get ready for the future and

learn how to use AI.

78. What does it mean for humans and AI to work together?
Human-AI symbiosis is a working partnership in which both parties make each other stronger. People bring creativity, morals, and compassion to the table, while AI brings accuracy and speed based on facts. This relationship makes people and machines work better together and make better decisions. It starts a new era of mutual growth instead of competition.

79. Is it possible for Agentic AI to produce discoveries on its own?
Yes, but only within certain limits. It can find patterns, make guesses, or come up with experiments based on data. Agentic AI has already discovered novel chemicals and genetic pathways in fields such as chemistry and genetics. But validation still needs people who know how to understand context and moral

issues.

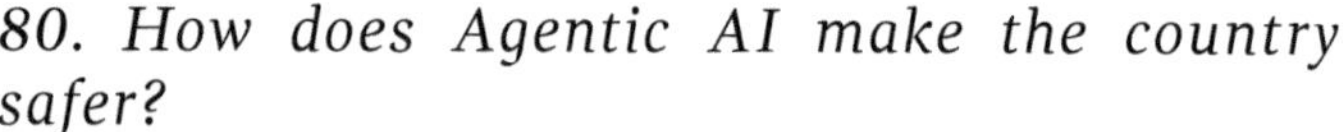

80. How does Agentic AI make the country safer?
It helps with monitoring, cybersecurity, and predictive defensive analytics. AI bots keep an eye on patterns, find risks, and set off quick responses. When used ethically, it makes intelligence operations and crisis management stronger. But misusing weapons or using them on their own raises significant moral and humanitarian issues that need stringent worldwide control.

"The measure of progress in Agentic AI is not how fast it learns, but how wisely it acts."

81. What does "situational awareness" mean in Agentic AI?

The system can see and understand what's going on around it in real time. Agentic AI keeps an eye on the situation, guesses what *will happen next, and changes its behaviour based on that. This feature is essential for self-driving cars, drones, and robots that work in changing and unpredictable environments.*

82. How may Agentic AI help make things more equal?
By making individualised digital services available to everyone, we can ensure that everyone has access to quality education, healthcare, and jobs. Agentic AI can help those who don't have access to services, translate languages, and customise learning materials. But fair infrastructure and ethical oversight are necessary to make sure that automation helps everyone, not just a small group of people.

83. What does "meta-learning" mean in Agentic AI?
"Learning to learn," or meta-learning, allows AI to improve at learning on its own. It improves algorithms based on what it has learned before, which makes it easier to adapt

to new jobs. This self-optimisation is similar to how people can adapt, and it is essential for enabling intelligent systems to function in a wide range of real-world situations that are difficult to foresee.

84. How can Agentic AI fight false information?

Using language and visual analysis, AI agents can check facts, find the sources of false information, and spot deepfakes. They help the media, teachers, and lawmakers tell the truth by checking information against dependable databases. But AI needs to stay open so that it doesn't get censored or misused in content moderation.

85. What part does Agentic AI play in running things?

Governments utilise it to help citizens, decide how to use resources, and judge policies. It makes things easier, cuts down on corruption, and clarifies matters. AI agents can, for example, keep an eye on public projects or handle the distribution of welfare. But governance needs protections to eliminate prejudice in algorithms and the misuse of people's data.

86. Can Agentic AI show interest?

It is feasible to design artificial curiosity to seek new information or make exploration more efficient. Agents pretend to be curious to make learning more efficient and find new solutions more quickly. But it's algorithmic, not emotional; it has mathematical aims instead of real curiosity or inner desire as people have.

87. What effect does Agentic AI have on starting a business?

AI agents assist business owners with market research, product design, and customer interaction encouragement. They can make judgments independently, recognise trends, and run their businesses on their own. This makes it easier for new businesses to get started and encourages new ideas, which helps companies proliferate. Using innovative, flexible automation solutions is becoming increasingly crucial for business success.

88. Can Agentic AI make public health better?
Yes. It keeps an eye on disease patterns, improves hospital management, and gets patients more involved. It keeps track of how infections spread and what resources are needed during pandemics. AI-powered diagnostics like Qure.ai and PathAI enable doctors to make faster, more accurate treatment decisions, saving lives by providing real-time, data-driven medical assistance.

89. What is the most essential thing that Agentic AI can't do?
It doesn't have a mind or the ability to think about right and wrong. It can analyse and make decisions, but it doesn't understand context or morality the way people do. Relying on training data makes it harder to be creative and fair.

AI's decisions still need human oversight to make sure they are guided, understood, and morally sound.

90. What is the relationship between Agentic AI and cloud ecosystems?
Agentic AI can get to massive datasets and scalable processing capacity through APIs and distributed computing. AI agents in the cloud work together across borders to help with education, industry, and government around the world. Integration enhances real-time analytics, enables continuous learning, and makes it safer for autonomous systems to share data.

"Agentic AI brings us closer to machines that don't just obey — they understand."

91. Can Agentic AI make things easier for individuals with disabilities to use?

Yes. It gives power to adaptive technologies like voice recognition, screen readers, and systems that can read emotions. AI agents tailor *support for students or workers with disabilities to help them communicate, navigate, and participate more successfully. Inclusive AI ensures that everyone can use it and feel empowered, regardless of their abilities.*

92. How can Agentic AI help protect the environment?

By looking at ecosystems, forecasting deforestation, and making the best use of energy. AI drones keep an eye on animals, and predictive agents look at climatic concerns. Governments use these kinds of systems to monitor pollution and manage water and farming in a way that is good for the environment and follows the law.

93. What does quantum computing have to do with Agentic AI?

Quantum computing makes Agentic AI much more potent by significantly increasing processing speeds. It lets you solve complex problems that current computers can't, such as protein folding or financial modelling. The combination offers agents that are faster, smarter, and capable of analysing massive, complex datasets with never-before-seen precision.

94. How does Agentic AI change the way customers interact with businesses?

It makes services more personal, guesses what people want, and automates help through natural interactions. Chatbots, recommendation algorithms, and virtual assistants keep people engaged around the clock. Agentic AI learns from every conversation, which makes customers happier and more loyal while also lowering expenses in fields like retail and education.

95. Can AI that is agentic take the place of human intuition?

No. It can imitate logic and prediction, but it doesn't have the emotional depth, empathy, or moral sense that people do. Intuition entails the subconscious integration of experiences, a process that AI cannot emulate. But it can help people make better judgments by providing data-backed insights that complement their intuition.

96. What part will Agentic AI play in schooling for life?
It will be a personal learning partner that keeps track of goals, finds resources, and provides feedback that adapts based on your needs. AI mentors that change as their skills improve will help lifelong learners by making education ongoing and tailored to their needs. This will help close the gap between school, work, and personal growth.

97. How does Agentic AI make sure that decisions are fair?
By putting fairness limits in place and keeping an eye out for bias in training data and models. Ethical audits and algorithmic transparency

help find and fix patterns of discrimination. Fair AI design ensures that the results are fair to people of all genders, races, and income levels.

98. How will Agentic AI affect how people work together around the world?
It connects academics, teachers, and innovators across languages and time zones. AI translators, project managers, and data-sharing platforms make it possible for people all across the world to work together in real time. Agentic AI accelerates scientific discoveries, education, and diplomacy by encouraging everyone to collaborate. This helps cultures make progress together.

99. Is it possible for Agentic AI to become aware?
Science says no right now. Consciousness necessitates self-awareness, emotions, and subjective experience, none of which robots possess. Agentic AI imitates reasoning and

adaptability but lacks internal perception. It is still a tool, not a living being, even though there are still discussions about AI ethics and philosophy.

100. What will happen to Agentic AI in the future?
Agentic AI will become an essential companion in all areas of life, learning, and business. Its future is in responsible intelligence, which means finding a balance between freedom and morality, and speed and compassion. When guided by human principles, Agentic AI can help people reach their full potential and transform our understanding of progress toward a more sustainable and inclusive future.

"The magic of Agentic AI is not in its code, but in its capacity to co-create with us."

Books By The Same Author

Scan Here
FOR QUALITY BOOKS
For Home Library for
Parents, Educators &Students

About The Author

Dr Dheeraj Mehrotra, Head of Training and Education at Adani GEMS Education and Research Institute, Mumbai, India, is a distinguished educational leader and innovator with over three decades of experience transforming education through excellence and innovation. A recipient of the President of India's National Teacher Award (2006), recommended by the Council For The Indian School Certificate Examinations (CISCE), he is a certified expert in Six Sigma (White and Yellow Belt), Neuro-Linguistic Programming (NLP), and Total Quality Management (TQM). His specialisation encompasses academic audits, school quality assurance and accreditation (SQAA), and the implementation of Kaizen and 5S in schools. As an accomplished author, Dr Mehrotra has published over 200 books on various subjects, including computer science, artificial intelligence, digital body language, quality circles, and school management. His contributions also include the development of more than 150 free educational mobile apps for teachers, students, and parents, a feat recognised by the Limca Book of Records and the India Book of Records. Dr Mehrotra has served as Principal at prestigious institutions such as De Indian Public School in New Delhi, NPS International School in Guwahati, and Kunwar's Global School in Lucknow. He has also held the position of Education Officer at GEMS in Gurgaon, making significant contributions to the global education community. As a premier UDEMY instructor, Dr Mehrotra has created over 500 courses that have impacted more than 800,000 learners across 180 countries. As the Founder Chairman of the IoT Society of India, he also advocates for the integration of technology in education worldwide. He was recently appointed as a mentor for the National Mission for Mentoring (NMM), the National Council for Teacher Education (NCTE), Government of India.

www.authordheerajmehrotra.com